To Dear Grandma 1965
From

W9-BBF-559

To Dear Gregory, 1965.
From Gramma & Grampa.

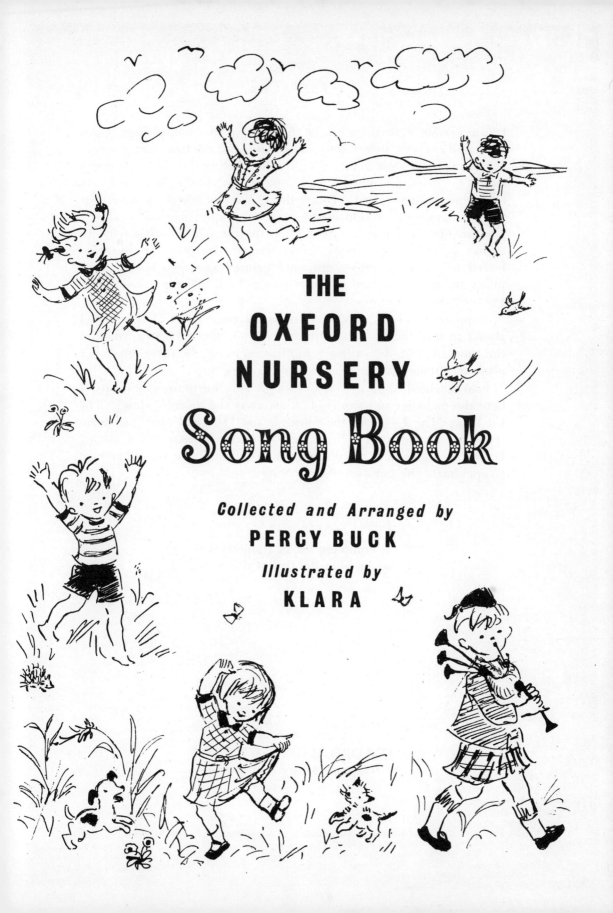

THE
OXFORD
NURSERY
Song Book

Collected and Arranged by
PERCY BUCK

Illustrated by
KLARA

PREFACE

It is as certain as anything can be that every reader who glances at this book will exclaim, before long, 'But that is not the tune (and possibly not the words) to which I am accustomed'. Before the blame for this is laid at my door, I would ask such a person to choose, at hazard, any title from my index, and then ask the first dozen friends he meets for their remembered version of the song. His experience will certainly astonish him, and may create a sympathy for one who has tried to collate a hundred specimens. Every song in this book has been referred to children, grown-ups, and printed versions, both for its music and its words; and in but few cases have I been persuaded that any orthodox text exists.

Being thus driven to choose between alternatives, I have tried always to take the least sophisticated version, and then to harmonize the tunes so that the ordinary mother or nurse, however small her piano-technique, may be able to 'keep things going'.

I am indebted to Messrs. J. Curwen & Sons for permission to print here the melodies and words of 'Blow away the morning dew', 'The Cuckoo', 'The Frog and the Mouse', and 'This old Man', all from 'English Folk Songs for Schools', edited by Cecil Sharp and S. Baring Gould, which book I can recommend to children who are old enough to appreciate the beauties of Folk Song.

P.C.B.

A complete list of contents will
be found at the end of this book.

Music Department

OXFORD UNIVERSITY PRESS

44 CONDUIT STREET · LONDON W.1

Reproduced and printed lithographically by N.V. Gebr. Keesmaat, Haarlem (Holland)

A RING, A RING O' ROSES

1. A ring, a ring o' ro-ses A pocket full of po-sies. Cu-sha! Cu-sha! All fall down.

2. The King has sent his daughter
To fetch a pail of water.
Cusha! Cusha!
All fall down.

3. The robin on the steeple
Is singing to the people.
Cusha! Cusha!
All fall down.

4. The wedding bells are ringing,
The boys and girls are singing.
Cusha! Cusha!
All fall down.

A, B, C, TUMBLE-DOWN D

A, B, C, Tum-ble-down D, The Cat's in the cupboard, and can't see me.

© Copyright 1933, Oxford University Press. Renewed in U.S.A. 1961

© Illustrated Edition 1961, Oxford University Press

Printed in Holland

BLOW AWAY THE MORNING DEW

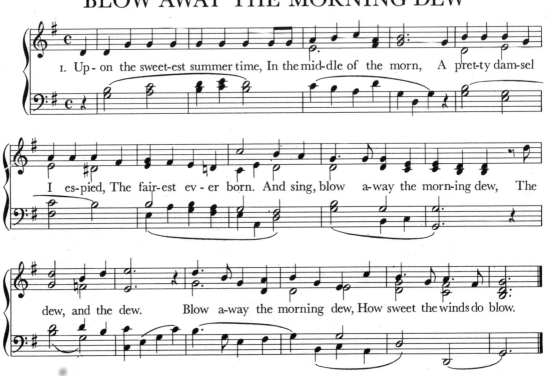

1. Up-on the sweet-est summer time, In the mid-dle of the morn, A pret-ty dam-sel I es-pied, The fair-est ev-er born. And sing, blow a-way the morn-ing dew, The dew, and the dew. Blow a-way the morning dew, How sweet the winds do blow.

2. The yellow cowslip by the brim,
   The daffodil as well,
   The timid primrose, pale and trim,
   The pretty snowdrop bell.
   And sing, etc.

3. She's gone with all those flowers sweet,
   Of white, of red and blue,
   And unto me about my feet
   Is only left the rue.
   And sing, etc.

Melody and Words from *English Folk Songs for Schools*, collected and edited by Cecil Sharp and S. Baring Gould. Curwen Edition, No. 6051. Reprinted by permission of J. Curwen & Sons, Ltd.

BAA, BAA, BLACK SHEEP

Baa, baa, black sheep, have you a-ny wool? Yes sir, yes sir, three bags full.

One for the master, and one for the dame, But none for the lit-tle boy that lives down the lane.

I LOVE LITTLE PUSSY

Fairly slowly

1. I love lit-tle pus-sy, Her coat is so warm, And if I don't hurt her She'll do me no harm.

2. I'll not pull her tail,
   And won't drive her away,
   But Pussy and I
   Together will play.

3. She'll sit by my side,
   And I'll give her some food,
   And she'll like me, because
   I am gentle and good.

4

TURN AGAIN, WHITTINGTON

Turn a-gain, Whit-ting-ton, Thou wor-thy ci - ti-zen, Lord Mayor of Lon-don.

When this tune is very well known it should be sung as a round for 3 voices, the 2nd singer entering at bar 3, the 3rd singer at bar 5.

THREE CHILDREN SLIDING ON THE ICE

1. Three child-ren slid - ing on the ice, All on a sum-mer's day,____ As

it fell out, they all fell in, The rest__ they ran a - way.____

2. Now had these children been at home,
   Or sliding on dry ground,
   Ten thousand pounds to one penny
   They had not all been drowned.

3. You parents all that children have,
   And you that have got none,
   If you would have them safe abroad,
   Pray keep them safe at home.

THE MILLER OF THE DEE

From 'Love in a Village' 1762

17th Century Air

Fairly quickly

1. There was a jol-ly mil-ler once lived on the riv-er Dee; He danced and sang from morn till night, No lark so blithe as he. And this the bur-den of his song for ev-er used to be. I care for no-bo-dy, no, not I, if no-bo-dy cares for me.

2. I live by my mill, God bless her! She's my kindred, child, and wife;
I would not change my station for any other in life.
No lawyer, surgeon, or doctor e'er had a groat from me:
I care for nobody, no, not I, if nobody cares for me.

3. When spring begins its merry career, oh! how his heart grows gay!
No summer's drought alarms his fears, nor winter's sad decay.
No foresight mars the miller's joy, who's wont to sing and say:
Let others toil from year to year — I live from day to day.

4. Thus like the miller, bold and free, let us rejoice and sing:
The days of youth are made for glee, and time is on the wing.
This song shall pass from me to thee, along this jovial ring:
Let heart and voice and all agree to say long live the king.

MARY, MARY, QUITE CONTRARY

Ma-ry, Ma-ry, quite con-tra-ry, How does your gar-den grow, __ With sil - ver bells and cock - le shells And pret-ty maids all in a row.

ONE MAN WENT TO MOW

One man went to mow, went to mow a meadow, One man went to mow, went to mow a meadow.

In this song verse 2 is 'Two men went to mow', up to v. 10 'Ten men went to mow'. In bar 3 the numbers are counted backwards– *e.g.* in v. 5 the third bar is 'five men, four men, three men, two men, one man went to mow.'

THE FROG AND THE MOUSE

1. There was a frog lived in a well, Whip-see did-dle dee dan-dy dee. There was a mouse lived in a mill, Whip-see did-dle-dee dan-dy dee. This frog he would a-woo-ing ride, With sword and buck-ler by his side, With a har-um scar-um, did-dle dum dar-um, Whip-see did-dle dee dan-dy dee.

2. He rode till he came to Mouse's Hall,
Where he most tenderly did call,
'O Mistress Mouse, are you at home?
And if you are, O pray come down!'

3. 'My uncle Rat is not at home,
I dare not for my life come down.'
Then Uncle Rat he soon comes home,
'And who's been here since I've been gone?'

4. 'Here's been a fine young gentleman,
Who swears he'll have me if he can.'
Then Uncle Rat gave his consent,
And made a handsome settlemen

Melody and Words from *English Folk Songs for Schools*, collected and edited by Cecil Sharp and S. Baring Gould. Curwen Edition, No. 6051. Reprinted by permission of J. Curwen & Sons, Ltd.

THE KEEL ROW

Tyneside Ballad

1. As I cam' in by Sand - gate, by Sand - gate, by Sand - gate, As I cam' in by Sand - gate, I heard a las - sie sing! O! weel — may the keel row, the keel row, the keel — row, O! weel — may the keel row, that my dear lad - die's in.

2. He wears a gude blue bonnet, blue bonnet, blue bonnet.
He wears a gude blue bonnet, and dimpled is his chin.
Then weel may the keel row, the keel row, the keel row,
O! weel may the keel row, that my dear laddie's in.

3. O! who is like my Johnny, my Johnny, my Johnny,
O! who is like my Johnny, 'mong lads o'coaly Tyne.
O! weel may the keel row, etc.

4. He'll sing and dance so lightly, so lightly, so lightly,
He'll sing and dance so lightly, and oh! that he were mine.
O! weel may the keel row, etc.

LITTLE MISS MUFFET

Lit-tle Miss Muf-fet sat on a tuf-fet, Eat-ing curds and whey;—— There

came a great spi-der, and sat down be-side her, And frightened Miss Muf-fet a - way.

LITTLE TOMMY TUCKER

Little Tommy Tucker sang for his sup-per; What shall we give him, but white bread and but-ter?

How can he cut it, with-out an-y knife? How can he mar-ry, with-out an-y wife?

HUSH-A-BYE, BABY

Rather slowly

Hush-a-bye, Ba - by, on the tree-top, When the wind blows, the cra - dle will rock.

When the bough breaks the cra-dle will fall, And down will come cradle, and ba-by, and all.

DANCE A BABY DIDDY

Dance a ba - by did - dy, ___ What can mammy do wid' e? ___

Sit in her lap. Give it some pap, And dance a ba - by did - dy. ___

DING DONG BELL

Ding dong bell ! Pus-sy's in the well ! Who put her in ? Lit-tle Tommy Green.

Who pulled her out ? Little Tommy Stout. What a naughty boy was that To drown poor pussy cat, Who

ne'er did a-ny harm, But killed all the mice in his fa-ther's barn.

NUTS IN MAY

Here we go ga-ther-ing nuts in May, nuts in May, nuts in May ;

Here we go ga-ther-ing nuts in May, on a cold and fros-ty morn-ing.

ONE, TWO, BUCKLE MY SHOE

One, two, Buck-le my shoe, Three, four, O-pen the door,

Five, six, Pick— up sticks, 7, 8, Lay— them straight,

9,   10,   A good— fat hen,   11,   12,   Dig— and delve,

13,   14,   Maids— a-court-ing,   15,   16,   Maids in the kitch-en,

17,   18,   Maids a-wait-ing,   19,   20,   My plate's emp-ty!

DRINK, PUPPY, DRINK

Words and music by G. J. Whyte Melville

Here's to the fox in his earth be-low the rocks; And here's to the line that we fol-low; And here's to the hound with his nose up-on the ground, Tho' mer-ri-ly we whoop and we hol-loa!

CHORUS

Then drink, pup-py, drink, and let ev-'ry pup-py drink That is old e-nough to lap and to swal-low; For he'll

grow in-to a hound, so we'll pass the bot-tle round, And merrily we'll whoop and we'll holloa!

LITTLE BOY BLUE

Lit-tle Boy Blue, Come blow up your horn, The sheep's in the meadow, the cow's in the corn.

Where's the boy that looks af-ter the sheep? He's un-der the hay— cock, fast a-sleep.

Will you wa-ken him? No, not I, For if I do— he's sure to cry.

THREE LITTLE KITTENS,
THEY LOST THEIR MITTENS

1. Three lit-tle kit-tens, they lost their mit-tens, So they be-gan to cry,— 'O mo-ther dear, come here, come here, for we have lost our mit-tens.' 'Lost your mit-tens? You naugh-ty kit-tens! Then you shall have no

2. Three little kittens, they found their mittens,
   So they began to cry,
   'O mother dear, come here, come here,
   For we have found our mittens'.
   'Found your mittens? you good little kittens,
   Now you shall have some pie.'
   'Prrrr! Prrrr!
   Now we shall have some pie.'

THREE BLIND MICE

Three blind mice, See how they run! — They all ran af-ter the far - mer's wife, Who cut off their tails with a carv - ing knife, Did you ev - er see such a thing in your life As three blind mice.

This can be sung as a round for 3 voices, but when this is done the first 2 bars must be sung 3 times, 'see how they run' 3 times, and the final 2 bars count as part of the 'second time through'.

LONDON'S BURNING

Lon-don's burn-ing, Lon-don's burn-ing, Fetch the en - gines, Fetch the en - gines, Fire! Fire! Fire! Fire! Pour on wa - ter, pour on wa - ter.

When this tune is very well known, it should be sung as a round for 4 voices, each singer entering when the one before has sung 2 bars.

HOT-CROSS BUNS

Hot-cross buns! Hot-cross buns! One a penny, two a penny, Hot-cross buns!

If you have no daughters, Give them to your sons; One a penny, two a penny, Hot-cross buns!

THE LINCOLNSHIRE POACHER

Words and music traditional

1. When I was bound ap-pren-tice in fa-mous Lin-coln-shire, —— I served my ma-ster tru-ly for near-ly sev-en long year, —— Till I took up with poach-ing, as you shall quick-ly hear; For it's my de-light of a shi-ny night in the sea-son of the year. ——

2. As me and my companions were setting of a snare,
   The gamekeeper was watching us, for him we did not care;
   For we can wrestle and fight, my boys, and jump out anywhere;
   For it's my delight of a shiny night in the season of the year.

3. As me and my companions were setting four and five,
   And taking of them up again, we took the hare alive;
   We popped her into a bag, my boys, and through the wood did steer;
   For it's my delight of a shiny night in the season of the year.

4. We threw her o'er our shoulders, and wandered through the town,
   We called inside a neighbour's house, and sold her for a crown;
   We sold her for a crown, my boys, but I did not tell you where;
   For it's my delight of a shiny night in the season of the year.

5. Well, here's success to poaching, for I do think it fair;
   Bad luck to ev'ry gamekeeper that would not sell his deer;
   Good luck to ev'ry housekeeper that wants to buy a hare;
   For it's my delight of a shiny night in the season of the year.

HEY DIDDLE, DIDDLE, THE CAT AND THE FIDDLE

Hey diddle, diddle, The cat and the fiddle, The cow jumped o-ver the moon;— The

lit-tle dog laughed to see such sport, And the dish ran a-way with the spoon.

THE OWL AND THE PUSSY-CAT

1. The Owl and the Pussy- Cat went to sea In a beauti- ful pea-green boat, They took some honey, and

plen-ty of money, Wrapped up in a five-pound note. The Owl looked up to the stars a - bove, And

Hey Diddle, Diddle melody reprinted by permission of Messrs. Novello & Co., Ltd.

sang to a small gui - tar, 'O love - ly Pus-sy, O Pus-sy, my love, What a

beau - ti - ful pus - sy you are!' _____ 'O love - ly Pus - sy, O

Pus - sy, my love, What a beau - ti - ful pus - sy you are!' _____

2. Pussy said to the Owl, 'You elegant fowl!
   How charmingly sweet you sing!
   O let us be married, too long we have tarried:
   But what shall we do for a ring?'
   They sailed away for a year and a day,
   To the land where the Bong-tree grows,
   And there in a wood a Piggy-wig stood,
   With a ring at the end of his nose.

3. 'Dear Pig, are you willing to sell for one shilling
   Your ring?' Said the Piggy 'I will'.
   So they took it away, and were married next day
   By the Turkey who lives on the hill.
   They dined on mince, and slices of quince,
   Which they ate with a runcible spoon;
   And hand in hand, on the edge of the sand,
   They danced by the light of the moon.

Poem by Edward Lear.
Reprinted by permission of the copyright owners, Frederick Warne & Co., Ltd., London.

MULTIPLICATION IS VEXATION

Mul - ti - pli - ca - tion is vex - a - tion, Div - i - sion is as bad, ___ The
rule of three doth puz - zle me, And prac - tice drives me mad.

THE NORTH WIND DOTH BLOW

Not too fast

The North wind doth blow, And we shall have snow, And
what will the Ro - bin do then, poor thing? He'll sit in the barn, And
keep him- self warm, And hide his head un - der his wing, poor thing.

LADYBIRD, LADYBIRD, FLY AWAY HOME

La - dy - bird, La - dy - bird, fly a - way home, Your

house is on fire, and your chil - dren are gone. Fly a - way, La - dy - bird,

fly a - way home, Your house is on fire, and your chil - dren are gone.

LAVENDER'S BLUE

1. Lav-en-der's blue, diddle, diddle, Lav-en-der's green, When I am King, diddle, diddle, You shall be queen.

2. Call up your men, diddle, diddle,
   Set them to work,
Some to the plough, diddle, diddle,
   Some to the cart.

3. Some to make hay, diddle, diddle,
   Some to cut corn,
While you and I, diddle, diddle,
   Keep ourselves warm.

4. Lavender's green, diddle, diddle,
   Lavender's blue,
If you love me, diddle, diddle,
   I will love you.

JOHN PEEL

J. W. Graves

Old Cumberland Air

1. D'ye ken John Peel with his coat so gay? D'ye
Chorus For the sound of his horn brought me from my bed, And the

ken John Peel at the break o' day? D'ye ken John Peel when he's
cry of his hounds, which he oft-times led; Peel's 'view halloo' would

Repeat for Chorus

far, far a-way With his hounds and his horn in the morn — ing?
wa-ken the dead, Or the fox from his lair in the morn — ing.

2. Yes, I ken John Peel and Ruby too,
  Ranter and Ringwood, Bellman and True;
  From a find to a check, from a check to a view,
  From a view to a death in the morning.
    For the sound of his horn, etc.

3. Then here's to John Peel from my heart and soul,
  Let's drink to his health, let's finish the bowl;
  We'll follow John Peel through fair and through foul,
  If we want a good hunt in the morning.
    For the sound of his horn, etc.

4. D'ye ken John Peel with his coat so gay?
  He liv'd at Troutbeck once on a day;
  Now he has gone far, far away;
  We shall ne'er hear his voice in the morning.
    For the sound of his horn, etc.

WHERE ARE YOU GOING TO,
MY PRETTY MAID?

1. 'Where are you going to, my pretty maid? Where are you going to, my pretty maid?' 'I'm go-ing a-milk-ing, Sir', she said, 'Sir', she said, 'Sir', she said, 'I'm go-ing a-milk-ing, Sir', she said.

2. 'May I go with you, my pretty maid?'
'Yes, if you please, kind Sir', she said.

3. 'What is your fortune, my pretty maid?'
'My face is my fortune, Sir', she said.

4. 'Then I can't marry you, my pretty maid.'
'Nobody asked you, Sir', she said.

YOUNG LAMBS TO SELL

'Young lambs to sell, young lambs to sell', If I'd as much mo-ney as I could tell, I nev-er would cry, 'Young lambs to sell, young lambs to sell.'

v. 2 'Old chairs to mend' and 'as I could spend'.

BYE, BABY BUNTING

Softly, and getting softer all through

Bye, Ba - by Bunt - ing, Dad - dy's gone a - hunt - ing, To

get a lit - tle rab - bit-skin To wrap the Ba - by Bunt - ing in.

Bye, Ba - by Bunt - ing, Bye, Ba - by Bunt - ing.

THE SPIDER AND THE FLY

'Won't you walk in-to my parlour?' said the spider to the fly, 'It's the prettiest lit-tle par - lour you

ev - er did es - py. And the way in - to my par - lour is   up a wind - ing stair, And

I have ma - ny pret - ty things to   show you when we're there'. 'O   no, no,' said the lit - tle fly, 'to

ask me is   in vain, For   who goes up the wind - ing stair will   not come down a - gain'.

SAVEZ-VOUS PLANTER LES CHOUX?

1. Sa - vez - vous plan - ter   les choux,   A   la mo - de, à   la

mo - de, Sa - vez - vous plan - ter   les choux,   A   la mo - de de   chez nous?

2. On les plante avec le pied
   A la mode de chez-nous.

3. On les plante avec la main
   A la mode de chez-nous.

OH DEAR, WHAT CAN THE MATTER BE?

Quickly

1. Oh dear! What can the mat-ter be? Dear, dear! What can the mat-ter be?

Oh dear! What can the mat-ter be? John-ny's so long at the Fair.——— He

(End here)

promised he'd buy me a fairing should please me, And then for a kiss Oh! he vowed he would tease me; He

(Go back to beginning)

promised he'd bring me a bunch of blue rib-bons To tie up my bon-ny brown hair.

2. He promised he'd bring me a basket of posies,
   A garland of lilies, a garland of roses,
   A little straw hat, to set off the blue ribbons
   That tie up my bonnie brown hair.

PAT-A-CAKE, PAT-A-CAKE, BAKER'S MAN

Pat - a - cake, pat - a - cake, ba - ker's man, Bake me a cake as fast as you can.

Prick it, and pat it, and mark it with B, And toss it up high for ba - by and me.

SEE-SAW, MARJORIE DAW

See - saw, Mar - jo - rie Daw, John - ny shall have a new mas - ter;

He shall have but a pen - ny a day, Be - cause he can't work a - ny fast - er.

OVER THE HILLS AND FAR AWAY

1. Tom he was a pi-per's son, He learnt to play when he was young; But
all the tunes that he could play Was 'O-ver the hills and far a-way.'
O-ver the hills and a great way off, The wind shall blow my top-knot off.

2.
Tom with his pipe made such a noise
That he pleased both the girls and the boys;
Who always stopped to hear him play
'Over the hills and far away'
Over, etc.

NEEDLES AND PINS

Nee-dles and pins! Nee-dles and pins! When a man's married his trou-ble be-gins.

FRERE JACQUES

Frè - re Jac - ques, Frè - re Jac - ques, dor - mez vous? dor - mez vous?

Son - nez les mat - i - nes, Son - nez les mat - i - nes, Din din don, din din don.

This song is intended to be sung as a Round for 2, 3, or 4 singers. Each singer must begin two bars after his predecessor, and each should sing the complete verse 2 or 3 times (as may be arranged). The singer who comes in last will thus be left with two bars to sing alone, and the pianist must be prepared to finish at the same time.

GEORGY PORGY

Geor - gy Por - gy, pud - ding and pie, kiss'd the girls and made them cry;

When the boys came out to play, Geor - gy Por - gy ran a - way, ran — a - way.

OH WHERE, AND OH WHERE IS MY LITTLE DOG GONE?

Oh where and oh where is my lit-tle dog gone? Oh where and oh where can he be?

With his ears cut short, and his tail cut long, Oh where, oh where is he?_____

PETER PIPER

Pe-ter Pi-per picked a peck of pic-kled pep-per, Pe-ter Pi-per picked a peck of pic-kled pep-per.

If Peter Pi-per picked a peck of pickled pep-per, Where's the peck of pickled pepper Pe-ter Piper picked?

PEASE PUDDING HOT

Pease pudding hot, pease pudding cold, Pease pudding in the pot, nine days old.

Some like it hot, some like it cold, Some like it in the pot, nine days old.

LITTLE BO-PEEP

1. Lit-tle Bo-peep has lost her sheep, And can't tell where to find them;

Leave them a - lone, and they'll come home, And bring their tails_ be - hind them.

2. Little Bo-peep fell fast asleep,
   And dreamt she heard them bleating;
   But when she awoke she found it a joke,
   For they were still a-fleeting.

3. Then up she took her little crook,
   Determined for to find them; [bleed,
   She found them indeed, but it made her heart
   For they'd left their tails behind them.

4. She heaved a sigh and wiped her eye,
   And ran over hill and dale, O,
   And tried what she could, as a shepherdess should,
   To tack to each sheep its tail, O.

ORANGES AND LEMONS

'Oranges and Le-mons' says the bells of St. Cle-men's; 'You owe me five

farthings' says the bells of St. Mar-tin's; 'When will you pay me?' says the

bells of Old Bai-ley; 'When I grow rich' says the bells of Shore-

-ditch; 'When will that be?' says the bells of Step-ney; 'I do not

Smoothly

know' says the great bell of Bow.   Here comes a can-dle to_ light you to

staccato

bed,   And here comes a   chop-per, to_ chop off your head.

HERE WE GO ROUND THE MULBERRY BUSH

I. Here we go round the mul-berry bush, the mul-berry bush, the mul-berry bush.

Here we go round the mul-berry bush, on a cold and fros-ty morn-ing.

2. This is the way we wash our hands.

3. This is the way we brush our hair.

4. This is the way we brush our clothes.

5. This is the way we go to school.

6. This is the way we come home from school.

THIS LITTLE PIG WENT TO MARKET

This lit - tle pig went to mar - ket, This lit - tle pig stayed at home,

This lit - tle pig__ had roast beef, This lit - tle pig__ had none, And

this lit - tle pig__ said 'Wee, wee, wee, wee, wee', All the way home.

WHO KILLED COCK ROBIN?

1. Who killed Cock Ro-bin? I, said the sparrow, with my bow and arrow, I killed Cock

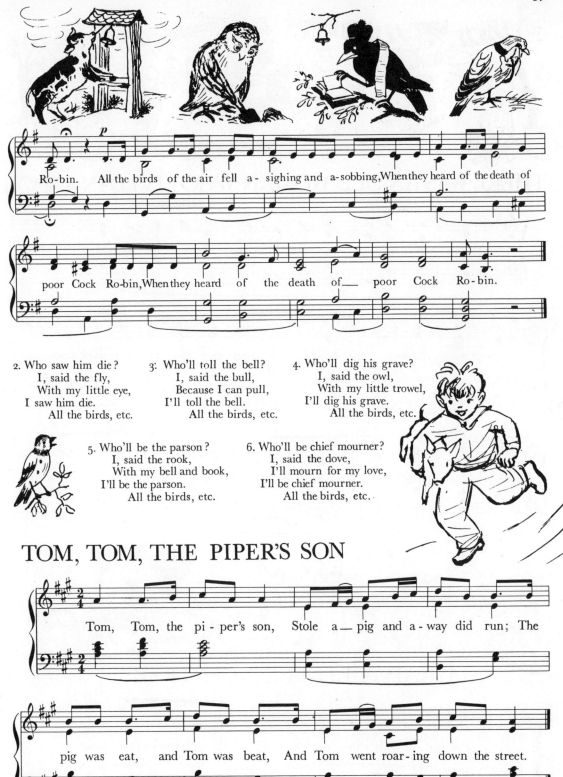

Ro-bin.　All the birds of the air fell a-sighing and a-sobbing, When they heard of the death of

poor Cock Ro-bin, When they heard of the death of___ poor Cock Ro-bin.

2. Who saw him die?
   I, said the fly,
   With my little eye,
   I saw him die.
      All the birds, etc.

3. Who'll toll the bell?
   I, said the bull,
   Because I can pull,
   I'll toll the bell.
      All the birds, etc.

4. Who'll dig his grave?
   I, said the owl,
   With my little trowel,
   I'll dig his grave.
      All the birds, etc.

5. Who'll be the parson?
   I, said the rook,
   With my bell and book,
   I'll be the parson.
      All the birds, etc.

6. Who'll be chief mourner?
   I, said the dove,
   I'll mourn for my love,
   I'll be chief mourner.
      All the birds, etc.

TOM, TOM, THE PIPER'S SON

Tom, Tom, the pi-per's son, Stole a___pig and a-way did run; The

pig was eat, and Tom was beat, And Tom went roar-ing down the street.

THERE WAS AN OLD WOMAN WHO LIVED IN A SHOE

There was an old wo-man who lived in a shoe, She
had so ma-ny children she didn't know what to do; She gave them some broth, with-
-out an-y bread, Then she whipped them all round, and sent them to bed.

I HAD A LITTLE NUT-TREE

I had a lit-tle nut - tree, no-thing would it bear

But a sil - ver nut - meg and a gold-en pear. The King of Spain's daugh - ter

came to vis - it me, And all___ for the sake of my lit - tle nut - tree.

JACK AND JILL

1. Jack and Jill went up the hill to fetch a pail of wa-ter; Jack fell down and broke his crown, And Jill came tumbling af-ter.

2. Up Jack got, and home did trot,
As fast as he could caper;
He went to bed to mend his head
With vinegar and brown paper.

THE CUCKOO

1. The cuck-oo is a pretty bird, She sing-eth as she flies; She bring-eth us good ti-dings, She tell-eth us no lies; She suck-eth all sweet flow-ers To keep her throt-tle clear, And ev-'ry time she sing-eth Cuck-oo! Cuck-oo! Cuck-oo! The sum-mer draw-eth near.

2. The Cuckoo is a giddy bird,
    No other is as she,
That flits across the meadow,
    That sings in every tree.
A nest she never buildeth,
    A vagrant she doth roam;
Her music is but tearful —
        Cuckoo!
'I nowhere have a home.'

3. The Cuckoo is a witty bird,
    Arriving with the spring.
When summer suns are waning
    She spreadeth wide her wing.
She flies th'approaching winter,
    She hates the rain and snow;
Like her, I would be singing
        Cuckoo!
And off with her I'd go.

From *English Folk Songs for Schools*, collected and edited by Cecil Sharp and S. Baring Gould Curwen Edition, No. 6051. Reprinted by permission of J. Curwen & Sons, Ltd.

LITTLE JACK HORNER

Lit-tle Jack Horn-er sat in a cor - ner, Eat-ing a Christ-mas pie; —— He put in his thumb, and pulled out a plum, And said 'What a good boy am I.'

LITTLE POLLY FLINDERS

Lit-tle Pol-ly Flin-ders sat among the cin - ders, Warm-ing her pretty lit-tle toes; Her mother came and caught her, and smacked her lit-tle daughter, For spoiling her nice new clothes.

TEN LITTLE NIGGER BOYS

1. Ten lit-tle nigger boys went out to dine,—One o-ver-ate himself, and then there were nine.

Nine lit-tle nig-ger boys stay-ing up late, One o-ver-slept himself, and then there were eight.

2. Eight little nigger boys went down to Devon,
   One went and lost himself, and then there were
      seven.
   Seven little nigger boys chopping up sticks,
   One chopped himself in half, and then there
      were six.

3. Six little nigger boys, playing near a hive,
   A bumble bee stung one, and then there were five.
   Five little nigger boys, playing on the shore,
   A big wave drowned one, and then there were four.

4. Four little nigger boys went upon the sea,
   A big whale swallowed one, and then there
      were three.
   Three little nigger boys went to the Zoo,
   A polar bear hugged one, and then there
      were two.

5. Two little nigger boys, sitting in the sun,
   One got frizzled up, and then there was one.
   One little nigger boy, living all alone,
   He got married, and then there were none.

42

POLLY-WOLLY-DOODLE

American

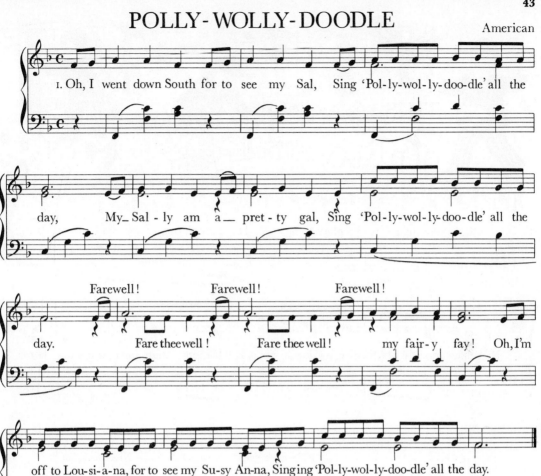

1. Oh, I went down South for to see my Sal, Sing 'Pol-ly-wol-ly-doo-dle' all the day, My Sal-ly am a pret-ty gal, Sing 'Pol-ly-wol-ly-doo-dle' all the day. Farewell! Farewell! Farewell! Fare thee well! Fare thee well! my fair-y fay! Oh, I'm off to Lou-si-a-na, for to see my Su-sy An-na, Singing 'Pol-ly-wol-ly-doo-dle' all the day.

2. Oh, my Sal, she am a maiden fair,
 Sing 'Polly-wolly-doodle' all the day,
With laughing eyes an' curly hair,
 Sing 'Polly-wolly-doodle' all the day,
 Fare thee well, etc.

3. Oh, I came to a river an' I couldn't get across,
 Sing 'Polly-wolly-doodle' all the day,
An' I jumped upon a nigger, for I thought he
 was a hoss,
 Sing 'Polly-wolly-doodle' all the day,
 Fare thee well, etc.

4. Oh, a grasshopper sittin' on a railroad track,
 Sing 'Polly-wolly-doodle' all the day,
A-pickin' his teef wid a carpet tack,
 Sing 'Polly-wolly-doodle' all the day,
 Fare thee well, etc.

5. Behind de barn, down on my knees,
 Sing 'Polly-wolly-doodle' all the day,
I thought I heard a chicken sneeze,
 Sing 'Polly-wolly-doodle' all the day,
 Fare thee well, etc.

6. He sneezed so hard wid de whoopin' cough,
 Sing 'Polly-wolly-doodle' all the day,
He sneezed his head an' his tail right off,
 Sing 'Polly-wolly-doodle' all the day,
 Fare thee well, etc.

THIS OLD MAN

1. This old man, he played one, He played nick-nack on my drum;
Nick-nack, pad-dy whack, give a dog a bone, This old man came roll-ing home.

2. This old man, he played two,
He played nick-nack on my shoe;
Nick-nack, etc.

3. This old man, he played three,
He played nick-nack on my tree;
Nick-nack, etc.

4. This old man, he played four,
He played nick-nack on my door;
Nick-nack, etc.

5. This old man, he played five,
He played nick-nack on my hive;
Nick-nack, etc.

6. This old man, he played six,
He played nick-nack on my sticks;
Nick-nack, etc.

7. This old man, he played seven,
He played nick-nack down in Devon;
Nick-nack, etc.

8. This old man, he played eight,
He played nick-nack on my gate;
Nick-nack, etc.

9. This old man, he played nine,
He played nick-nack on my line;
Nick-nack, etc.

10. This old man, he played ten,
He played nick-nack on my hen;
Nick-nack, etc.

Melody and Words from *English Folk Songs for Schools*, collected and edited by Cecil Sharp and S. Baring Gould. Curwen Edition, No. 6051. Reprinted by permission of J. Curwen & Sons, Ltd.

THE MAN IN THE MOON

The man in the moon came down too soon, And asked the way to Nor-wich; He went by the South, and burnt his mouth With eat - ing cold plum por - ridge.

POLICHINELLE

1. Pan! qu'est-c'qu'est là? C'est Po - lich - in - elle, Mam'sel - le, Pan! qu'est-c'qu'est

End here

là? C'est Po - lich - inelle que v'là. Il est mal fait, Et

craint de vous dé - plai - re, Mais il es - pè - re Vous chan - ter son coup - let.

1. Il est mal fait,
   Et craint de vous déplaire,
   Mais il espère
   Vous chanter son couplet.
   Pan! etc.

2. Toujours joyeux,
   Il aime fort la danse,
   Il se balance
   D'un petit air gracieux.
   Pan! etc.

3. A vous faire vivre,
   Mes enfants, il aspire,
   Jeunes et vieux,
   Ceux qui vivent sont heureux.
   Pan! etc.

J'AI DU BON TABAC

J'ai du bon ta-bac dans ma ta - ba - tiè - re, J'ai du bon ta-bac, tu n'en au - ras

pas. J'en ai du fin, et du bien râ - pé, Ce n'est pas pour ton vi - lain

nez. J'ai du bon ta-bac dans ma ta - ba - tiè - re, J'ai du bon ta-bac, tu n'en au - ras pas.

SAINT PAUL'S STEEPLE

Up - on Paul's Stee-ple stands a tree, As full of ap - ples as may be, The

lit - tle boys of Lon-don Town, They run with hooks to pull them down, And

then they run from hedge to hedge, Un - til they come to Lon - don Bridge.

SUR LE PONT D'AVIGNON

Sur le Pont d'Avig - non L'on y danse, L'on y danse, Sur le Pont d'Avignon

(End here) (Without time)*

L'on y danse tout en rond. Les beaux messieurs font comm' ca; Et puis encore, comm' ça.

*The children, while singing this recitative, should imitate how the fine gentlemen dance, substituting other names in each subsequent verse: *e.g.* Monsieur le Maire, les blanchisseuses, les gendarmes, les soldats, les ga-mins, etc. etc.

OLD KING COLE

Old King Cole was a mer-ry old soul, And a mer-ry old soul was

he, He called for his pipe, and he called for his bowl, And he

called for his fid - dlers three. Ev - 'ry__ fid-dler had a

fid-dle so__ fine, And a ve-ry fine__ fid - dle had he, O there's

none so rare as can com-pare With King Cole and his fid-dlers three.

Other verses are usually added, in which the King calls for different members of his band: *e.g.* harpers, drummers, trumpeters, etc.

A FROG HE WOULD A-WOOING GO

1. A Frog he would a - woo-ing go, Heigh - ho says Row-ley; A

Frog he would a - woo-ing go, Whether his mo-ther would let him or no. With a

Row - ley, Pow - ley, Gammon and Spinach, Heigh-ho, says An-to-ny Row-ley.

2. Then off he set, in his opera hat,
    Heigh-ho, etc.
   And on the way he met a rat.

3. Together they came to the mouse's hall,
   And there they did both knock and call.

4. But while they where all merry-making,
   A Cat and her Kittens came tumbling in.

5. The Cat she seized the rat by the crown,
   And the Kittens they pulled the little mouse down.

6. The frog ran home and was crossing a brook
   When a lily-white duck came and gobbled him up.

7. So that was the end of one, two, three,
   The rat and the mouse and the little frogee.

COCKLES AND MUSSELS

Unknown

Old Irish Air

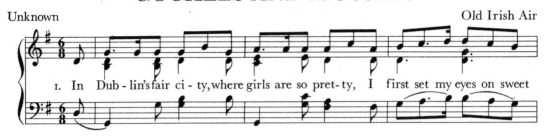

1. In Dub-lin's fair ci-ty, where girls are so pret-ty, I first set my eyes on sweet

Mol-ly Ma-lone, As she wheel'd her wheel-bar-row through streets broad and nar-row, Crying,

CHORUS

'Cock-les and mus-sels! A-live, a-live oh! A-live, a-live oh! A-

-live, a-live oh!' Cry-ing, 'Cock-les and mus-sels, a-live, a-live oh!'

2. She was a fishmonger, but sure 'twas no wonder,
   For so were her father and mother before;
   And they each wheeled their barrow through streets broad and narrow,
   Crying, 'Cockles and mussels, alive, alive oh!
   Alive, alive oh!' etc.

3. She died of a faver, and no one could save her,
   And that was the end of sweet Molly Malone;
   Her ghost wheels her barrow through streets broad and narrow,
   Crying, 'Cockles and mussels, alive, alive oh!
   Alive, alive oh!' etc.

SING A SONG OF SIXPENCE

Briskly

1. Sing a song of sixpence, A pocket full of rye, Four and twenty blackbirds baked in a pie.

When the pie was opened the birds began to sing, Wasn't that a dainty dish to set before the King?

2. The King was in his counting-house, counting out his money,
The Queen was in the parlour, eating bread and honey,
The maid was in the garden, hanging out the clothes,
When up came a blackbird, and pecked off her nose.

MARY HAD A LITTLE LAMB

Not too slowly

1. Ma-ry had a lit-tle lamb, Its fleece was white as snow, And ev-'ry-where that Ma-ry went The lamb was sure to go. ⎯ He followed her to school one day, That was a-gainst the rule,⎯ It made the chil-dren laugh and play To see a lamb at school.

3. 'What makes the lamb love Mary so?'
    The eager children cry;
'O, Mary loves the lamb, you know',
    The teacher did reply.
And you each gentle animal
    In confidence may bind,
And make them follow at your call,
    If you are always kind.

2. And so the teacher turned him out,
    But still he lingered near,
And waited patiently about
    Till Mary did appear.
And then he ran to her, and laid
    His head upon her arm,
As if to say 'I'm not afraid,
    You'll keep me from all harm'.

HARK, HARK, THE DOGS DO BARK

Not too slowly

Hark, Hark, the dogs do bark, The beg-gars are com-ing to town,

Some in rags, and some in tags, and some in vel-vet gown.

HUMPTY DUMPTY

Hump-ty Dump-ty sat on a wall, Hump-ty Dump-ty had a great fall;

All the King's horses and all the King's men Could-n't put Humpty to-ge-ther a-gain.

YANKEE DOODLE

American

1. O, Yan-kee Doo-dle went to town, Up-on a lit-tle po - ny, And there he saw the
men and boys all eat-ing ma-ca-ro - ni. Yan-kee Doodle, keep it up, Yan - kee Doodle
Dan - dy; Mind the mu-sic and the step, And with the girls be han - dy.

2. And there we saw a thousand men
   As rich as Squire David;
   And what they wasted every day,
   I wish it could be savèd.
   (Chorus)

3. It scared me, so I hooked it off,
   Nor stopped, as I remember,
   Nor turned about, till I got home
   Into my mother's chamber.
   (Chorus)

THERE WAS A LITTLE MAN,
AND HE HAD A LITTLE GUN

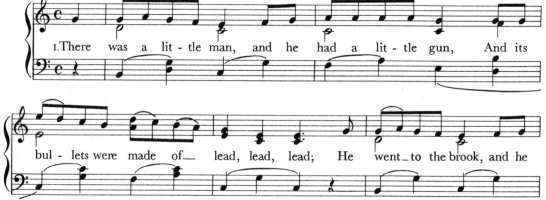

1. There was a lit - tle man, and he had a lit - tle gun, And its
bul - lets were made of— lead, lead, lead; He went—to the brook, and he

shot a lit-tle duck, And he shot_ it _ right through the head, head, head.

2. He took it home to his old wife Joan,   And sent him to look once more in the brook,
   Who started a fire to make, make, make,   And bring back home the drake, drake, drake.

OLD MOTHER HUBBARD

1. Old Mo-ther Hub-bard, she went to the cup-board, to fetch the poor dog — a

bone;— When she got there, the cupboard was bare, And so the poor dog had none. —

(3 times)

2. She went to the ba-ker to buy him some bread, But when she got back, the poor dog was dead.
3. She went to the join-er to buy him a coffin, But when she got back, the poor dog was laughing.
4. The dame made a curt-sey, the dog made a bow, The dame said 'Your servant', the dog said 'Bow-wow.'

LOCH LOMON'

Scottish Melody

1. By yon bon-nie banks and by yon bon-nie braes, When the sun shines bright on Loch Lo-mon', Where

CHORUS

me and my true love were ev-er wont to gae, On the bonnie, bonnie banks o' Loch Lo - mon'. O

ye'll tak' the high road, and I'il tak' the low road, And I'll be in Scot-land a-fore ye, But

me an' my true love will nev-er meet a-gain, On the bon-nie, bon-nie banks o' Loch Lo - mon'.

2. 'Twas there that we parted in yon shady glen,
   On the steep, steep side o' Ben Lomon',
   Where in purple hue, the Hieland hills we view,
   And the moon comin' out in the gloamin'.
       O ye'll tak' the high road, etc.

3. The wee birdies sing and the wild flowers spring,
   And in sunshine the waters are sleeping;
   But the broken heart it kens nae second spring,
   Tho' the waefu' may cease frae their greeting.
       O ye'll tak' the high road, etc.

LONDON BRIDGE IS BROKEN DOWN

Not too slowly

1. Lon - don Bridge is bro - ken down, Dance o - ver my La - dy Lea!

Lon - don Bridge is bro - ken down, With a gay La - dy. ____

2. How shall we build it up again?
3. Build it up with silver and gold.
4. Silver and gold will be stolen away.
5. Build it up with iron and steel.
6. Iron and steel will bend and bow.
7. Build it up with wood and clay.
8. Wood and clay will wash away.
9. Build it up with stone so strong,
   Dance over my Lady Lea!
   Hurrah! it will last for ages long,
   With a gay lady.

GOOSEY, GOOSEY GANDER

Goosey, Goosey Gander, Whither shall I wan-der? Upstairs and downstairs And in my Lady's chamber.

There I met an old man Who wouldn't say his prayers, So I took him by the left leg And threw him down the stairs.

Mrs. BOND

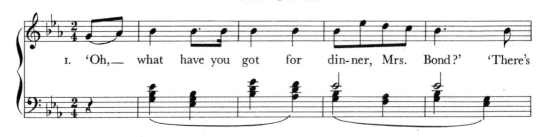

1. 'Oh,— what have you got for din-ner, Mrs. Bond?' 'There's

beef— in the lar-der and ducks in the pond'. Dil-ly, dil-ly, dil-ly, dil-ly,

come and be killed, For you— must be stuffed and my cus-tom-ers filled.

2. 'Pray send first the beef in for dinner, Mrs Bond,
And then dress the ducks that are swimming in the pond.'
Dilly, etc.

3. 'John Ostler, go fetch me a duckling or two.'
'That I will', says John Ostler, 'I'll try what I can do.'
Dilly, etc.

4. 'I have been to the ducks that are swimming in the pond,
But none of them will come to be killed, Mrs Bond.'
Dilly, etc.

5. Mrs Bond rushed down to the pond in a rage,
With lots and lots of onions and lots and lots of sage.
Dilly, etc.

O MY LITTLE SIXPENCE

1. O my lit-tle six-pence! I love six-pence! I love six-pence bet-ter than my life;

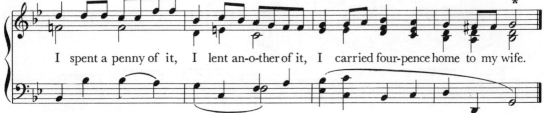

I spent a penny of it, I lent an-o-ther of it, I carried four-pence home to my wife.

*The B flat in this chord must be B natural at the end of the last verse.

2. O my little fourpence! I love fourpence!
   I love fourpence better than my life;
   I spent a penny of it, I lent another of it,
   I carried twopence home to my wife.

3. O my little twopence! I love twopence!
   I love twopence better than my life;
   I spent a penny of it, I lent another of it,
   I carried nothing home to my wife.

4. O my little nothing! I've got nothing!
   I've got nothing for the rest of my life;
   I can spend nothing, I can lend nothing,
   But I love nothing better than my wife.

RUB-A-DUB-DUB, THREE MEN IN A TUB

Rub-à-dub-dub, Three men in a tub, And who d'you think they be?___ The but-cher, the ba-ker, the can-dle-stick ma-ker, So turn out the knaves, all three.

RIDE A COCK HORSE

Ride a cock horse to Ban-bu-ry Cross, To see a fine la-dy up-on a white horse,

Rings on her fin-gers, and bells on her toes, She shall have mu-sic where-ev-er she goes.

THE FOX JUMPED OVER THE PARSON'S GATE

Old Song

Old English Melody
(Twice)

1. The Hunts-man blows his horn in the morn, When folks goes hunt-ing, O! ___ When folks goes hunt - ing, O! ___ When folks goes hunt - ing, O! ___ But all my fan - cy dwells up-on Nan-cy, So I'll cry Tal - ly - ho! ___

2. The fox jumps over the Parson's gate,
   And the hounds all after him go.
   The hounds all after him go.
   But all my fancy, etc.

3. Now the Parson had a pair to wed
   As the hounds came full in view.
   The hounds came full in view.
   But all my fancy, etc.

4. He tossed his surplice over his head,
   And bid them all adieu!
   He bid them all adieu!
   But all my fancy, etc.

5. Oh! never despise the soldier-lad,
   Tho' his station be but low.
   Tho' his station be but low.
   But all my fancy, etc.

6. And if you ask me of this song
   The reason for to show,
   I don't exactly know-ow-ow
   But all my fancy, etc.

JACK SPRAT

In a firm march time

Jack Sprat could eat no fat, His wife could eat no lean; And so between them both you see They licked the platter clean.

I SAW THREE SHIPS COME SAILING BY

1. I saw three ships come sail - ing by, sail - ing by, sail - ing by, I

saw three ships come sail - ing by,— On Cris-si-mas Day in the morn - ing.

2. And what d'you think was in them then ?

3. Three pretty girls were in them then.

4. And one could whistle, and one could sing,
   And one could play on the violin;
Such joy there was at my wedding,
   On Crissimas Day in the morning.

THE MERMAID

Old Sea Song

Traditional Air

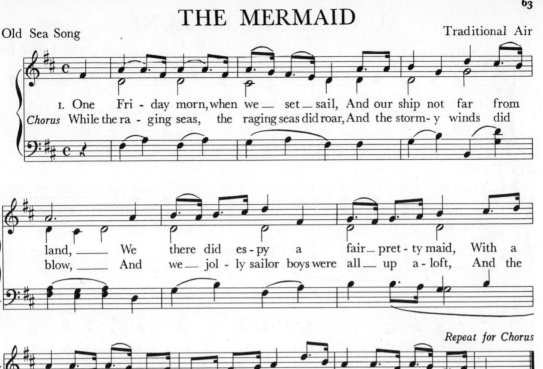

1. One Fri - day morn, when we — set — sail, And our ship not far from

Chorus While the ra - ging seas, the raging seas did roar, And the storm- y winds did

land, ___ We there did es - py a fair — pret - ty maid, With a

blow, ___ And we — jol - ly sailor boys were all — up a - loft, And the

Repeat for Chorus

comb and a glass — in her hand, her hand, her hand, With a comb and a glass in her hand.

land lubbers ly-ing down be-low, be-low, be-low, And the landsmen were all — down be-low.

2. Then up spake the captain of our gallant ship,
   And a gallant captain was he;
'I have married a wife in fair London town,
   And this night she a widow will be.'
      While the raging seas, etc.

3. And then up spake the little cabin-boy,
   And a fair-haired boy was he;
'I've a father and a mother in fair Portsmouth town,
   And this night they will weep for me.'
      For the raging seas, etc.

4. Then three times round went our gallant ship,
   And three times round went she;
For the want of a lifeboat they both went down,
   As she sank to the bottom of the sea.
      For the raging seas, etc.

AU CLAIR DE LA LUNE

Old French Air

Not too slowly

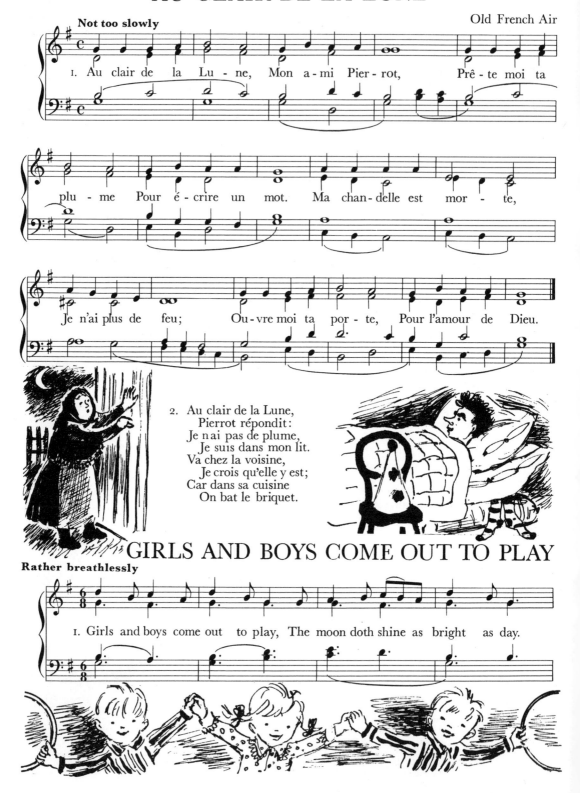

1. Au clair de la Lu - ne, Mon a - mi Pier - rot, Prê - te moi ta plu - me Pour é - crire un mot. Ma chan - delle est mor - te, Je n'ai plus de feu; Ou - vre moi ta por - te, Pour l'amour de Dieu.

2. Au clair de la Lune,
   Pierrot répondit:
Je n'ai pas de plume,
   Je suis dans mon lit.
Va chez la voisine,
   Je crois qu'elle y est;
Car dans sa cuisine
   On bat le briquet.

GIRLS AND BOYS COME OUT TO PLAY

Rather breathlessly

1. Girls and boys come out to play, The moon doth shine as bright as day.

Leave your sup-per and leave your sleep, And join your play-fel-lows in the street.

2. Come with a whoop, and come with a call,
Come with a good will or not at all.
Up the ladder and down the wall,
A penny loaf will serve us all.

PUSSY-CAT, PUSSY-CAT, WHERE HAVE YOU BEEN?

'Pus-sy-cat, pus-sy-cat, where have you been?' 'I've been up to Lon-don to look at the Queen'.

'Pus-sy-cat, pus-sy-cat, what did you there?' 'I caught a lit-tle mouse un-der her chair'.

TWINKLE, TWINKLE, LITTLE STAR

1. Twinkle, twinkle, lit-tle star, How I wonder what you are, Up a-bove the world so high,

Like a diamond in the sky; Twin-kle, twinkle, lit-tle star, How I won-der what you are.

2. When the blazing sun is gone,
When he nothing shines upon,
Then you show your little light,
Twinkle, twinkle, all the night.
    Twinkle, etc.

3. Then the traveller in the dark
Thanks you for your tiny spark.
Could he see which way to go
If you did not twinkle so?
    Twinkle, etc.

4. In the dark blue sky you keep,
And often through my curtains peep,
For you never shut your eye
Till the sun is in the sky.
    Twinkle, etc.

CURLY LOCKS

Not too quickly

Cur - ly locks, Cur - ly locks, wilt thou be mine? Thou

shalt not wash dish - es, nor yet feed the swine, But sit on a cush-ion, and sew a fine seam, And feed up-on straw-ber-ries, su-gar, and cream.

DOCTOR FAUSTUS

Doc-tor Fau-stus was a good man, He whipped his schol-ars now and then;

When he whipped them he made them dance Out of Eng-land in-to France,

Out of France in-to Spain, And then he whipped them back a-gain.

HOW DOES MY LADY'S GARDEN GROW?

How does my la - dy's gar - den grow? How does my la - dy's gar - den grow? With

sil - ver bells and cock - le shell, And pret - ty maids all in a row.

THERE WAS A CROOKED MAN

There was a crook-ed man, And he went a crook-ed mile, And he

found a crook-ed six - pence Up-on a crook-ed stile; He bought a crook-ed cat, And it

caught a crook-ed mouse, And they all lived to-ge-ther in a crook-ed lit-tle house.

DANCE TO YOUR DADDY

Dance to your dad-dy, my — lit-tle lad-die, Dance to your dad-dy

my — lit-tle lamb. You shall have a fish-y on a lit-tle dish-y,

You shall have a fish-y when the boat comes in. Dance to your dad-dy,

my lit-tle lad-die, Dance to your dad-dy, my — lit-tle lamb.

WHAT ARE LITTLE BOYS MADE OF?

1. What are lit-tle boys made of? What are lit-tle boys made of?
Frogs and snails, and pup-py-dogs' tails,— That's what boys are made of.

2. What are little girls made of?
What are little girls made of?
 Sugar, and spice, and all things nice,
That's what girls are made of.

3. What are young men made of?
What are young men made of?
 Sighs, and leers, and crocodiles' tears,
That's what young men are made of.

4. What are young women made of?
What are young women made of?
 Ribbon, and laces, and sweet pretty faces,
That's what young women are made of.

TAFFY WAS A WELSHMAN

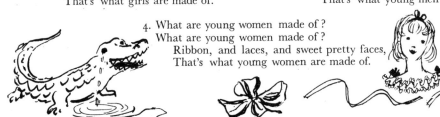

Taf-fy was a Welsh-man, Taf-fy was a thief,

Taf - fy came to my house and stole a leg of beef.— I—went to Taf- fy's house,

Taf - fy was from home, I re-turned the com-pli-ment, and stole a marrow bone.

SIMPLE SIMON

1. Sim - ple Si - mon met a pie - man go - ing to the fair,— Said

Sim - ple Si - mon to the pie - man, 'Let me taste your ware'.

2. Said the pieman unto Simon,
'Show me first your penny;'
Said Simple Simon to the pieman,
'Sir, I haven't any.'

3. Simple Simon went a-fishing,
For to catch a whale;
But all the water he had got
Was in his mother's pail.

4. Simple Simon went to look
If plums grew on a thistle;
He pricked his fingers in the leaves,
Which made poor Simon whistle.

HICKORY, DICKORY, DOCK

1. Hick-or-y, dick-or-y, dock! The mouse ran up the clock. The clock struck one, the mouse ran down, Hick-or-y, dick-or-y, dock!

2. Hickory, dickory, dare!
   The pig flew up in the air.
   The man in brown soon brought him down,
   Hickory, dickory, dare!

COCK-A-DOODLE-DO

1. Cock-a-doo-dle-do! My dame has lost her shoe, My mas-ter's lost his fidd-ling-stick, And does-n't know what to do.

2. Cock-a-doodle-do!
   My dame has found her shoe,
   My master's found his fiddling-stick,
   So Cock-a-doodle-do!

POP! GOES THE WEASEL

Up and down the Ci-ty Road, In and out the Ea-gle, That's the way the money goes, Pop! goes the wea-sel.

Half a pound of twopenny rice, Half a pound of treacle, That's the way the money goes, Pop! goes the weasel.

LUCY LOCKETT

Lu-cy Lock-ett lost her pock-et, Kit-ty Fish-er found it, But

ne'er a pen-ny was there in it, 'cept the bind-ing round it.

ONE MORE RIVER

Words and music American

1. Ole No - ah once he built de ark, Dar's one more rib - ber to cross; And patched it up wid hick - 'ry bark, Dar's one more rib - ber to cross.

CHORUS

One more rib - ber, An' dat's de rib - ber of Jor - dan; One more rib - ber, Dar's one more rib - ber to cross.

2. He went to work to load his stock,
He anchor'd de ark wid a great big rock

3. De animals went in one by one,
De elephant chewin' a caraway bun.

4. De animals went in two by two,
De rhinoceros an' 'de kangaroo.

5. De animals went in three by three,
De bear, de flea, an' de humble-bee.

6. The animals went in four by four,
Ole Noah got mad an' holler'd for more.

7. De animals went in five by five,
Wid Saratoga trunks they did arrive.

8. De animals went in six by six,
De hyena laughed at de monkeys' tricks.

9. De animals went in seven by seven,
Said de ant to de elephant, who are you a-shovin'?

10. De animals went in eight by eight,
Dey came wid a rush 'cause 'twas so late.

11. De animals went in nine by nine,
Ole Noah shouted, 'Cut dat line'.

12. De animals went in ten by ten,
De ark she blow'd her whistle den.

13. And den de voyage did begin,
Ole Noah pulled de gang-plank in.

14. Dey nebber know'd whar dey were at,
Till de ole ark bumped on Ararat.

15. De ole ark landed high and dry,
De baboon kissed de cow good-bye.

16. Now please just look out for de text,
To be continued in our next.

DAME, GET UP AND BAKE YOUR PIES

1. Dame, get up — and bake your pies, Bake your pies, bake your pies, Dame, get up — and bake your pies, — On Christ-mas Day in the morn - ing.

2. Dame, what makes your maidens lie?

3. Dame, what makes your ducks to die?

4. Their wings are cut, they cannot fly

THERE WAS A LADY LOVED A SWINE

Fairly fast

1.There was a la-dy loved a swine, 'Hon - ey' said she; 'Pig — hog, wilt thou be mine?' 'Hunc,' said he.

2. 'I'll build for thee a silver sty.
Honey,' said she;
'And within it thou shalt lie.'
'Hunc', said he.

3. 'All fastened with a silver pin,
Honey,' said she;
'That thou mayest go out and in.'
'Hunc', said he.

4. 'O tell me, wilt thou have me now,
Honey?' said she;
'Answer, or my heart will break.'
'Hunc', said he.

POLLY PUT THE KETTLE ON

Fairly quickly

Pol-ly put the kettle on, Pol-ly put the kettle on, Pol-ly put the kettle on, We'll all have Tea.

Su-key take it off a-gain, Su-key take it off a-gain, Su-key take it off a-gain, They're all gone a-way.

WHEN JOHNNY COMES MARCHING HOME

Old English Air

1. When Johnny comes marching home a-gain, Hur-rah! — Hur-rah! We'll give him a hear-ty wel-come then, Hur-rah! — Hur-rah! The men will cheer, the boys will shout, The la-dies they will all turn out, And we'll all feel gay when Johnny comes marching home.

2. Get ready for the Jubilee,
We'll give the hero three times three,
The laurel wreath is ready now
To place upon his royal brow.
And we'll all, etc.

3. Let love and friendship on that day
Their best of treasure then display,
And let each one perform his part
To fill with joy the warrior's heart.
And we'll all, etc.

INDEX

	Page		Page
A, B, C, Tumble-down D	1	The Mermaid	63
A frog he would a-wooing go	49	The Miller of the Dee	5
A ring, a ring o'roses	1	Mrs. Bond	58
Au clair de la lune	64	Multiplication is vexation	22
Baa, baa, black sheep	3	Needles and pins	30
Blow away the morning dew	2	The North wind doth blow	22
Bye, Baby Bunting	26	Nuts in May	11
Cock-a-doodle-do	72	Oh dear, what can the matter be?	28
Cockles and mussels	50	Old King Cole	48
The Cuckoo	40	Old Mother Hubbard	55
Curly Locks	66	O my little sixpence	59
Dame get up and bake your pies	75	One man went to mow	6
Dance a baby diddy	10	One more river	74
Dance to your Daddy	69	One, two, buckle my shoe	12
Ding dong bell	11	Oranges and lemons	34
Doctor Faustus	67	Over the hills and far away	30
Drink, puppy, drink	14	Oh where and Oh where is my little dog gone?	32
The Fox jumped over the parson's gate	61	The owl and the pussy cat	20
Frère Jacques	31	Pat-a-cake, pat-a-cake, baker's man	29
The Frog and the Mouse	7	Pease pudding hot	33
Georgy Porgy	31	Peter Piper	32
Girls and boys come out to play	64	Polichinelle	45
Goosey, goosey gander	57	Polly put the kettle on	76
Hark, hark, the dogs do bark	53	Polly-wolly-doodle	43
Here we go round the mulberry bush	35	Pop! goes the weasel	73
Hey diddle, diddle, the cat and the fiddle	20	Pussy-cat, pussy-cat, where have you been?	65
Hickory, dickory, dock	72	Ride a cock horse	60
Hot cross buns	18	Rub-a-dub-dub, three men in a tub	60
How does my lady's garden grow?	68	Saint Paul's steeple	46
Humpty Dumpty	53	Savez-vous planter les choux?	27
Hush-a-bye, baby	10	See-saw, Marjorie Daw	29
I had a little nut-tree	38	Simple Simon	71
I love little pussy	3	Sing a song of sixpence	51
I saw three ships come sailing by	62	The spider and the fly	26
Jack and Jill	39	Sur le pont d'Avignon	47
Jack Sprat	62	Taffy was a Welshman	70
J'ai du bon tabac	46	Ten little nigger boys	42
John Peel	24	There was a crooked man	68
The keel row	8	There was a lady loved a swine	76
Ladybird, ladybird, fly away home	23	There was a little man, and he had a little gun	54
Lavender's blue	23	There was an old woman who lived in a shoe	38
The Lincolnshire poacher	19	This little pig went to market	36
Little Bo-peep	33	This old man	44
Little Boy Blue	15	Three blind mice	17
Little Jack Horner	41	Three children sliding on the ice	4
Little Miss Muffet	9	Three little kittens	16
Little Polly Flinders	41	Tom, Tom, the piper's son	37
Little Tommy Tucker	9	Turn again, Whittington	4
Loch Lomond	56	Twinkle, twinkle, little star	66
London Bridge is broken down	57	What are little boys made of?	70
London's burning	18	When Johnny comes marching home	77
Lucy Lockett	73	Where are you going to, my pretty maid?	25
The man in the moon	44	Who killed Cock Robin?	36
Mary had a little lamb	52	Yankee Doodle	54
Mary, Mary, quite contrary	6	Young lambs to sell	25

Printed by N.V. Gebr. Keesmaat, Haarlem, Holland

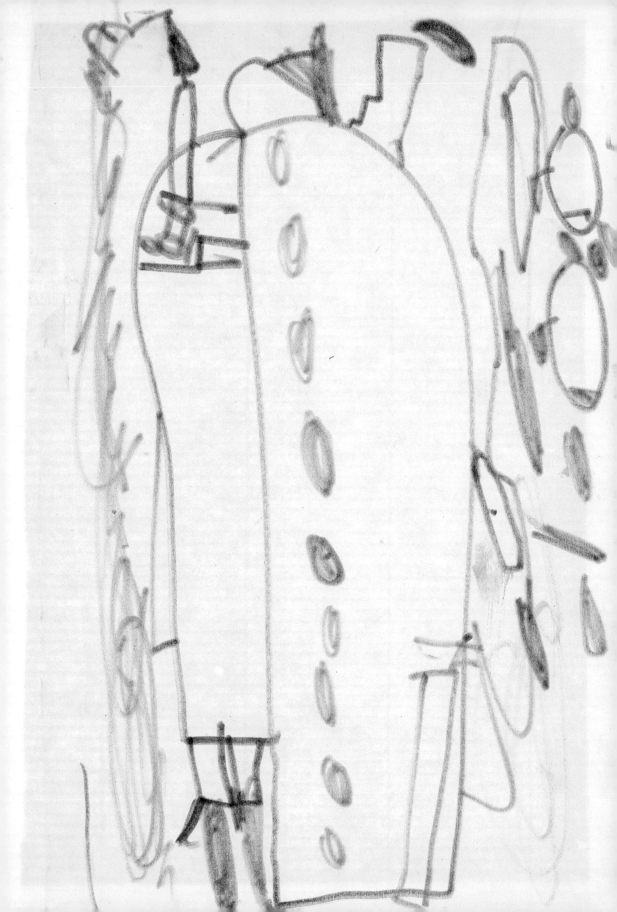